Living with Limits

Max Sinclair

and

Russell Bravo

A LION BOOK

Oxford · Batavia · Sydney

Text copyright © 1990 Max Sinclair and Russell Bravo
This edition copyright © 1990 Lion Publishing
All rights reserved

Published by
Lion Publishing Corporation
1705 Hubbard Avenue, Batavia, Illinois 60510, USA
ISBN 0 7459 1541 8
Lion Publishing plc
Sandy Lane West, Oxford, England
ISBN 0 7459 1541 8
Albatross Books Pty Ltd
PO Box 320, Sutherland, NSW 2232, Australia
ISBN 0 7324 0242 5

First edition 1990

All Bible quotations are from the *New International Version*

British Library Cataloguing in Publication Data
Sinclair, Max
    Living with limits.
    1. Physically handicapped persons. Self help
    I. Title
    362.4048

    ISBN 0-7459-1541-8

Printed and bound in Yugoslavia

Contents

1

Living with Limits

Almost every day I meet people who are living with limitations on their lives. The man pushing his disabled wife in a wheelchair. The partially deaf woman in a shop, trying to communicate with the shopkeeper.

My wife and I have a 25-year-old friend who is almost unable to speak. She looks down at the ground constantly, and becomes acutely distressed if she is not clinging tightly to the arm of one of her adoptive parents, who have cared for her ever since she was rescued from an emotionally horrific situation many years ago.

These people all have obvious disabilities. But I know many other people who have hidden limitations. These people have been hurt by life: perhaps by a broken relationship, a sense of failure, a feeling of inferiority, a lack of self-worth. For whatever reason, they have withdrawn into their own little world. Unseen bonds tie their hands and keep them from doing the things they want to do, from being the people they could be.

This book is for anyone who has limitations, seen or unseen, who wants to learn more about living a fulfilled life. It is also for people who would like to relate better to people with limitations.

I write from my own perspective as a person with limits. At the age of thirty-two, my spine was injured in a car crash. At first I was totally paralyzed from the neck down. After six months of hospital treatment and a year of therapy, I began to learn how to walk again and attempted to make my way back to relatively normal living.

It was a long, hard road. Today I remain partially paralyzed. The functioning of my right arm and leg is impaired, and each day I am aware of the various physical results of my injury.

I live with hidden limitations also. Any traumatic experience leaves its mark, whether psychologically, emotionally or mentally. I have made it a project to work on these areas as well.

Living with Limits is not an expert medical handbook; it is a practical approach born out of personal experience and nurtured by the invaluable advice of friends.

2

Shocking Reality

*'The X-rays show that you will never walk
again. I'm sorry.'*

*'I regret to have to tell you that your child
has muscular dystrophy. This is a degenerative
disease. He will not get better.'*

*'We have now tried everything possible. I'm
afraid we are not going to be able to save your
eyesight.'*

It is deeply shocking to receive that kind of
news. Even if you are tough. Even if you were
expecting it. Even if you had already thought
through some of the consequences.

The moment of realization repeats like an action replay in your mind. You relive it in nightmares, or sometimes in daydreams.

The new limits imposed on your life are permanent. They will not go away. You know it's true, but you don't want to believe it.

Life has changed irreversibly. Everything seems out of control. The bottom has fallen out of your world.

Fear invades your thinking. You can do nothing; there is no way you can escape. Events have overtaken you, and you have become an unwilling player in a real-life horror movie.

People's reactions vary. Some stare vacantly into space, totally unable to carry on with normal routines for a while. Some go through the usual motions, but with numbed hearts and paralyzed minds. Others express their grief through tears, tension, rage, or other open displays of emotion.

Shock is strange. It leads us to behavior and reactions that surprise us and those close to us. When we are in shock, we are not ourselves.

3

A Whole New Life-style

Some people live with limitations from the time of birth. Others find themselves suddenly hurled into a whole new world, where every aspect of life seems to be turned upside-down.

That's how I felt when I found myself in the hospital with a broken neck. Everyone around me — physiotherapists, occupational therapists, nurses, nurse aides — was dressed in uniform white. Doctors were easy to spot. Their white coats were usually flapping open.

There was a whole new language to learn. I was an Incomplete Lesion, Level C5. The contraption fitted to my head was called *tongs*

— something I had always associated with barbecues.

Routines were new. Each week a nurse came to my bedside and asked me to select my menu for the entire week ahead. Every day, three times a day, I had to gulp down an enormous quantity of pills. One day I counted twenty-seven.

Physiotherapists came twice daily to exercise everything I could move and to stretch everything I couldn't. Social workers called regularly, asking questions about my home and family.

And all this was just the beginning.

Coming to terms with this strange new world evoked a mixture of emotions. Part of me wanted to run away. Hide. Escape the stark, unpleasant reality I now found myself in.

Another part of me knew there was no way out, and tried bravely — with occasional success — to grasp that I had begun a new life which was not going to go away.

The whole world seemed upside down. There were a lot of questions to be answered.

Questions

Suddenly faced with limitations, some people bravely grit their teeth and act determined. Others shake a fist at life and shout, 'I'll beat this if it kills me.' Still others carry on quietly: hurt, puzzled and questioning.

There are the personal questions, through which we try to relate statistics to our own situation.

Why did the illness strike me?
Why was my car involved in the accident?
Why wasn't I somewhere else at the time?

Other questions stalking our minds are more
philosophical.

I don't deserve this, do I? Then why me?
Does God care?
Why does he allow this kind of trauma that has
  permanently limited my life?
Why doesn't he prevent this kind of thing?
Is God in control? Or is he powerless to control
  events in this world?

The questions mount up. We feel we need
answers in order to make sense of our
situation. We would feel more comfortable, we
think, if only we could see a purpose
behind our suffering, if only we could blame
someone or something.

  If we find no answers, we feel engulfed
in hopelessness. We feel we are spinning off
course, out of control. A sense of desolation
and fear creeps in.

  Are there any answers?

Turning to God

Some people turn to God for answers, and indeed the God of the Bible offers answers to many of our questions. But not to all of them.

The Bible tells us that the whole universe was started by a caring God, a God with personality and feelings. It assures us that this God is concerned with us as individuals. It also says, however, that we shall never understand everything completely.

If God cares at all, we may reason, he must be powerless to prevent suffering. Otherwise, why doesn't he step in and put an end to it?

But the Bible tells us God loved us so much that he created us free. Free to act independently. Free to distinguish right from wrong, to choose and be responsible for our choices. Free to succeed and fail, to fall and be picked up again.

Sadly, our world has used its freedom badly. It has rejected its creator, and it is now facing the consequences.

Humankind's decision to go its own way has brought death, disease and disaster to this world. And the evil that we have brought into the world attacks everyone — good people and bad people, people who deserve their fate and people who seem innocent.

God is broken-hearted about our suffering. But his way is not always to protect us from life's tragedies. Rather, he promises to stand by us, to help us through them.

God sent his own son, Jesus, into the confusion, pain and trauma of our world.

Born into poverty, Jesus devoted his short life to helping those in need. In the end, he was put to death by the authorities. He was crucified because he cared.

Jesus knew what it felt like to be alone and hurt. To be isolated and rejected. To feel physical, emotional and mental pain. To be misunderstood and let down. To have his life limited in a thousand ways that bite deep into the soul.

God understands how we feel. We can trust him, because he has identified with us by living our life. We can share our deepest experiences with him in confidence, knowing that he holds the answers to our many questions.

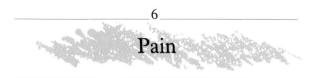

6

Pain

When we know that God is standing by us, we are better prepared for the battles we shall have to fight.

For some, there is physical pain. Whether temporary or permanent, pain is a grievously wearing companion. Every morning we may wake to the realization that its heavy hand will stalk each minute of the day and maybe haunt the night watches as well. This can cause despair.

Jesus' experience of physical pain was intense and agonizing. First he was whipped

with a cruel scourge. Then he was nailed
to a cross to die slowly of suffocation.

No less real is mental and emotional pain.
Feeling we have lost our purpose — at work,
in the family, in society — can cause an ache
as deep as any physical hurt.

Our circumstances have changed forever.
What we have lost will never return. We fight
a daily battle with our bewilderment at the
flight of established life patterns. Something
deep inside us has been fragmented. Whatever
used to maintain our balance has been toppled.

The emotional pain experienced by God
in sending his son Jesus to a certain death was
no less real. And for Jesus, the strain
of his task drove him to all-night, agonizing
prayer.

If we lose a loved one, a funeral marks
the occasion. A ceremony provides structure
for our grief. There is public recognition of the
passing.

But our loss has no such outlet. There is
no official ritual to give our tears a legitimate
channel. Society seems to require us to bear
our pain privately.

If I had not known that God was feeling
my pain with me, I might not have been able
to stand it.

7

Isolation

Pain is an isolating experience. It is something that only you are going through. Others are cut off from the inner sanctum where you wrestle with it, however much they may want to share that place with you.

Some people's well-meaning attempts to share your pain cause worse isolation. 'I understand how you feel,' they say, when in reality they can't.

Some people have said to me, 'At least you can be grateful for such and such.' There is little comfort in these words. Of course

I should be grateful for the good parts of my life, but that does not soothe the hurting parts.

'There are always others worse off than you' is another phrase sometimes used by misguided comforters. Your head tells you it's true. Your heart and soul insist that it's irrelevant. It does not solve the hurt.

Another little wedge is driven between you and someone who wants to help.

Looking fit and healthy can make matters worse. Outsiders comment that you look better, so you must be 'back to normal.' No one can see what is raging under the surface.

A healthy appearance may even widen the gap between your inner self and the outside world. Society gives us at most a few weeks in which to grieve. A brief period of grace, and then we are expected to be the same person we always were.

To meet these expectations, we learn to smile at the neighbors and control our tears and look calm. People will not understand if we continue looking glum. We have had time to fight our battle; we ought to have won by now. Deep inside, however, the battle continues.

When no one else seems to be puzzled, questioning, or involved in a struggle, the isolation seems worse. Surrounded by busy, smiling people, we must either crawl away and hide or come into the open and shout, 'Stop the world — I want to get off!'

Jesus knew how isolation feels. His followers deserted him. His friends turned against him. Alone, he faced suffering and death. Unlike many of our would-be comforters, he does understand exactly how we feel, and he offers his friendship when we are alone.

But for many, the isolation seems too great. The fact that others have found a way through seems irrelevant. Right now it is all too much. We want to escape.

8

Escape

Sooner or later we must face the fact that our limitations are permanent.

Most of us cannot handle all this means in a moment. It takes time to face the truth, let alone adapt and adjust to it. Rather than face our new situation, we want to run.

How we try to escape depends on what sort of person we are. Grief, despair and tears may be our reaction, especially if life has dealt us many difficult blows already.

Our reaction may be to try to ignore the problem altogether. I know a man who completely lost his eyesight, but refused to sell his car.

I can remember lying in the hospital, totally paralyzed from the neck down, telling friends I was looking forward to having more time to read and study over the next few months.

If we don't try to ignore the facts, we may still attempt to gloss over them, pretending that everything will soon be all right.

'I know I'm going to walk again,' spat out Mike from his wheelchair. 'I just know it. I am absolutely determined. I'll do it.' He had just been told that his spinal cord was severed, but his youthful optimism and gutsy determination shunned the facts he would eventually have to face.

Some of us feel the trauma so deeply that we consider the ultimate escape. Feelings of despair overwhelm us to a point where ending it all permanently seems the only way out.

'I thought about driving my car at high speed into a wall.'

'I pleaded with friends to get me some pills or something.'

Both these things have been said to me.

Probably many people consider this solution but never tell anyone.

It is not wrong to experience these feelings. They seem to be natural reactions. How we deal with them, however, is very important.

If we allow our feelings to take over, we may begin to live in another world, cut off from those around us. Moody, irritable and hard to live with, we test the patience of those who care about us most. Even in our escape world, something tells us that we are only postponing the day when we must face reality. In the meantime, we are hurting others.

Something also tells us that suicide is selfish. It might seem to solve our problems, but it leaves a trail of compounded misery and trauma for those who care about us.

'I looked at my child as she slept. Her innocent, trusting face made me realize I must not let her down,' a friend told me.

It is natural to want to escape, but we shall have to face things one day. Perhaps our biggest need is for someone to share our feelings with. Someone we can trust.

9

Sharing

Shock, bewilderment, and hurt are very private. It can be a lonely experience looking for the courage to stop running and face our new situation.

It is often painful to share our hurts even with those closest to us. The closer they are, the more hurt they will be by our pain. They need time to grieve just as we do.

Sharing the sad feelings can be hard, but we need to share. At some point we have to decide: are we going to retreat further into the relative safety of our private world and cut ourselves off from those who love us? Or shall we step out into the vulnerable place where we share our feelings?

Some of us find this step harder than others. We are afraid to show tears. We want people to think we are under control. We don't want our boiling inner frustration to be known.

Sharing our feelings may make us feel clumsy. Once spoken, words cannot be unsaid. We want to be sure we can trust those we share with. We want to know that our confidence will not be betrayed.

But sharing our inner world can be an immense relief. It begins to break down our sense of isolation. We are no longer fighting alone. Someone else cares. Someone else is trying to understand.

We were not made to live as isolated islands. A God of love designed us to love and be loved. This is why we feel the need for others to care.

Their caring may not be perfect, and their understanding will probably be inadequate. But we still need to share ourselves with them, because that is how we are designed.

The most meaningful help and comfort probably comes from family and friends who will just be there, without forcing us to talk, loved ones who will listen when we are ready to share.

The fact that they are with us and that they care gives a glimmer of hope that somehow we will get through.

Sharing will help us face the future, although it will not answer all our questions.

10

Time to Choose

A time comes when we must make choices.
Sometimes, in fact, we make choices without
realizing it. Our future direction is not
determined by fate. It is our choice. We can
choose how we respond to life's situations.

Will we choose to make the pain, isolation
and questioning caused by our hurt our
habitual life-style?

Or will we make our limitations a stepping
stone to something new?

Time alone is not the great healer some
people imagine. It allows emotions to settle. It

can help us face reality with clearer vision. It can give us space to re-evaluate life. But the mere passage of time does not heal anything. All it does is give us the opportunity to make choices.

An assortment of men shared my hospital ward ten years ago. Some were positive and optimistic then, but now are discouraged and bitter. Some were shocked and depressed, but now are cheerful and outgoing.

The simple passing of time did not make the difference. The difference was caused by the attitudes these men developed as they grappled with life's limits over the years.

The God who created us understands our feelings of anger, bitterness and frustration. He knows our listlessness, our low self-worth, the hopeless wave of despair that we sometimes feel crashing over our heads.

God does not limit his involvement to mere sympathy and understanding. He offers us a way to adjust to our new limits. A way to deal with our feelings. A basis for building a new life.

God does not force his way on anyone, but

he offers it to all. The time will come when we can move into a new dimension of living. It is time to choose.

11

Searching for Direction

When you start a new job, you may feel
apprehensive. There are new things to get used
to, new procedures to learn. Many companies
give new employees a handbook that explains
their vision. And ideally your supervisor is
available whenever you need further help.

Starting a new direction in life is like
that. It can be frightening, but there are
guides through the unfamiliar territory. Our
comprehensive handbook is the Bible. Our
sympathetic boss is Jesus.

Jesus is available whenever we need him.

He is interested not only in dealing with emergencies, but also in becoming closely involved with our day-to-day lives. He is utterly reliable.

Or maybe you prefer to see Jesus as an encouraging parent teaching a child to swim. The apprehensive, struggling learner feels all kinds of emotions. The concerned parent knows this, but continues to challenge and encourage the child. The parent knows that swimming is an important skill to acquire.

If the child trusts the parent, all will go well. As the child struggles to adjust to the water, the parent gives support and reassurance that there is purpose and hope in this experience.

Jesus is with us as we struggle too, reassuring us that there is hope in our experience. As we place our confidence in him, the bitter taste of meaninglessness fades away. In its place comes the sweet taste of purpose and peace.

Our quest for meaning, purpose and self-worth will find an answer. God says that you and I are infinitely valuable to him — not for what we can do, but because we are his creation. Our life has worth because he gave it to us.

The immense cost of Jesus' death also shows our value to God. The Bible tells us something that is hard to understand but wonderful to believe and accept: God gave up his son so that our messed-up lives could be put back together again. Jesus died so that we could live meaningful lives.

We may feel powerless, but God says we are not victims. Instead, we are people he cares about. Our life is not out of control; it is in his capable hands.

God may not change our circumstances, but he can alter our attitudes.

Attitudes

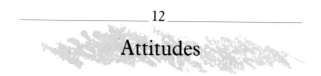

The Bible tells us that at the beginning of time each human being was in perfect harmony with God. Everyone was blissfully happy.

But something intruded into this happiness. First the humans' attitudes and then their actions went out of line with the maker's plan. This put them at odds with each other and with God.

We, like those early humans, also have problems with our attitudes. Not only are we at odds with each other and with God; we are not even comfortable with ourselves. We need to begin by looking at our attitudes, the key to our success in adjusting to life's difficulties. We shall not be able to move forward unless we look hard at where we are now.

Frustration and anger may rage within us. Limits frustrate us. Simmering resentment or blazing fury easily follow.

Bitterness may become a way of life with us if we think life has dealt us bitter blows.

Depression may result from our whirlpool emotions.

Guilt may arise if we know that some of our problems are our own fault. Or we may feel guilty at the way our situation affects others.

As we choose to move into a new dimension of living, we must deal with all these attitudes. We are not helpless victims. We are people God cares about.

When we know that God is standing by us, suffering with us, leading us where he wants us to go, we find our anger and depression slowly draining away.

God holds the solution to our negative attitudes. Even to the most hurtful of all — guilt.

God offers to deal with the guilt that dogs our footsteps. Some of our problems may be our own fault. We may also have hurt other people. But God offers forgiveness and peace of mind.

When Jesus died, our sin and guilt died with him. When Jesus awakened to a new life on Easter morning, he made it possible for us to have new life too. If we ask God to forgive us, he will get rid of our guilt. He will raise us to a new life of forgiveness, peace and purpose.

New Discoveries

Discovering this new foundation for living gives
us hope for the future. We now have a basis
for adjusting to our limits. This is not ill-founded
optimism. It is not pie in the sky.

It is new life in which someone cares for us.
Someone who is at the center of everything.
Someone who can make sense of life.

We might want to enjoy this new life im-
mediately, to receive it in a miraculous moment.
Certainly it begins in a moment in time,
a moment that we may be able to identify.

But our understanding of all that the new life
means will take much longer. For most people, the

experience of new life is a gradual growth.

I recently met a friend whose husband died suddenly of a heart attack. They had been very close. I asked gently, 'It happened two years ago — have you got over it now?'

Her reply surprised me. 'I don't think I shall ever get over it. But I am more adjusted to life without him.'

Even with permanent limits, we can find dignity and purpose. We can be content to be ourselves. We can accept our situation. We need to discover how best to use the time, talents, resources and qualities that God has given us.

As we discover the meaning of our new life, we embrace whatever part we can play. We happily accept this as God's new life-style for us.

This kind of adjustment is not easy, but it is possible. Enjoying God's friendship is the key. Traveling this new road with him as our guide, we find fulfillment. Words from Psalm 16 in the Bible express it well:

> *'You have made known to me the path of life; you will fill me with joy in your presence.'*

A New Look

Fresh discoveries will come thick and fast
as our life-style changes. Living with limits
will certainly bring new approaches in several
areas.

Our view of *work* will change. In our
society, work and employment have become
synonymous. The value of work is measured
by remuneration, and status is attached to
different kinds of employment.

God's view of work is different. Work
includes running a family, spending time with
people, praying, studying and so on. Work is

anything that contributes to building our own and other people's lives.

We will have new *leisure* activities too, new hobbies and ways of relaxing. For activities that are no longer possible, we will substitute new interests which renew us.

Our attitude to *friendship* may need to change. We sometimes wish we had more friends, not realizing that the key may lie with us. If you need a friend, be one.

As you take an interest in other people, they are naturally drawn to you. This is not a technique, but a way of living. It must be sincere.

Our preoccupation with our own problems diminishes as we reach out to others. Our feeling that we have a right to be understood changes into a concern to understand others.

15

Helping the Helpers

Living with limits includes learning to be dependent. Being helped isn't always easy. Helping isn't easy either, so we need to make sure we help the helpers.

Be patient. It is galling to realize that some things take us much longer than other people to achieve.

Because of hands that don't function well, I am constantly struggling with simple tasks like tying shoe laces. But I would rather take longer over something and manage it myself, than have everything done for me.

When someone seizes the laces, saying, 'Oh, let me help you,' I feel like exploding.

We need patience with those who want to help us but get it wrong. Most of us are not naturally patient. Fortunately, the Bible says that when God controls our lives, he will produce patience in us.

Be appreciative. 'Thank you' does not cost much, but it is always very important. It tells your helper you value him or her. If you forget to express thanks, your helper may wonder if you are ungrateful.

It is easy to take helpers for granted. We slip into thinking, 'That's what they are there for.' But even if they are paid helpers, never forget that they are choosing to help. Appreciating their choice is one small thing we can do to help them.

Be wise. Know what you can manage yourself and what you need help with. That requires wisdom. Sometimes it is worth struggling on your own. Sometimes it is wiser to seek help.

Once you have charted the different areas,

you will know where you are. Your helpers will also know. You will both feel secure.

God, give us grace to accept with serenity the things that cannot be changed, courage to change the things which should be changed, and the wisdom to distinguish the one from the other.
REINHOLD NIEBUHR

Manipulation: How to Avoid It

Some so-called 'friends' do not give friendship. They are people with needs of their own who want to use you.

People who feel intensely lonely or isolated may seek to gain attention and friendship by offering help to another person in need. Their 'help' is really manipulation.

Where I have been sure that this is the motive behind offered help, I have taken steps to ensure that I am not manipulated to satisfy someone else's need.

We need to find a firm but gentle way to

turn down inappropriate offers of help without personally rejecting would-be manipulators.

It is also good to see if something can be done to meet these people's real needs in a constructive way. Perhaps they could be referred to someone else who can work with them to sort out their problems.

One-time offers of inappropriate 'help' are different. While in a wheelchair, I was subjected to numerous toe-bruising, knuckle-crunching attempts by well-meaning passers-by who maneuvered me too swiftly through doors.

This was different from manipulative help, because once through the doors I was able to thank them heartily for their assistance and say goodbye!

Watch out for the manipulators, but don't get a phobia about them. They are people with needs, just like you and me.

Thanks for life!

People who cope with life's limits are an inspiration. One of my heroes is St. Paul in the Bible. In spite of the many difficulties he encountered, he still put gems like this in his letters: 'Give thanks in all circumstances.'

That was written by a man who suffered terribly, yet felt he had a lot to be thankful for. Notice he didn't say, 'Wait until you feel thankful,' or 'Wait until things get better.'

How can we be thankful when things are tough? How can we be thankful 'in all circumstances'?

Paul reveals an important secret: *Happiness does not depend on happenings.*

Someone whose life is placed in God's hands can be deeply thankful that God is present, even though plenty of uncomfortable things may be happening.

If you are in love with someone, if you have someone who really cares about you, then you can be thankful for all that this person means to you even while unpleasant things are going on around you.

No matter what is going wrong, you can still have deep joy in your relationship and confidence that this person will stay close to you through thick and thin.

If we love God, our relationship with him will be a great strength to us.

Paul did not hide from the pain in his life. He could not. But he could see that, with God's love, his life could be transformed. It could be renewed in the present, and totally restored in the future.

And Paul knew that, whatever his weakness, whatever his despair, nothing could stop God's love for him.